Alphabets of the World

Letters from 78 Languages

M. Schottenbauer, Ph.D.

DEDICATION

To my parents,

who encouraged me to write

many years ago.

Table of Contents

ACKNOWLEDGEMENTS

I am deeply grateful for the best of my education:

The guidance, support, advice

of my teachers, peers, and parents,

and also to the scholarship donors and my parents

who financially supported my long education.

Alphabets from Around the World

Alphabets from around the world have geometrically elaborate shapes! This book introduces 78 of the many alphabets from around the world, including common variations on letters. The purpose of this book is to provide interesting information for recreational use, not for formal reference.

This book is written primarily for English speakers who are unfamiliar with foreign alphabets. Comparisons are made to English only, and not among foreign alphabets. Foreign numerals are included in some, but not all languages presented here. Readers should note that some languages included do not have alphabets; in these cases, sample words or glyphs are provided. Also, some alphabets appear incomplete, containing letters with dotted circles indicating points of possible attachment to other letters in the same alphabet.

Languages from Europe

English

A	a
B	b
C	c
D	d
E	e
F	f
G	g
H	h
I	i
J	j
K	k
L	l
M	m
N	n
O	o
P	p
Q	q
R	r
S	s
T	t
U	u
V	v
W	w
X	x
Y	y
Z	z

Languages Overlapping with English

	Extra Letters		Omitted Letters	
Latin	Ā	ā	J	j
	Ē	ē	U	u
	Ī	ī	W	w
	Ō	ō		
	Ū	ū		
Italian	À	à		
	È	è		
	Ò	ò		
	Ù	ù		
Esperanto	Ĉ	ĉ	Q	q
	Ĝ	ĝ	W	w
	Ĥ	ĥ	X	x
	Ĵ	ĵ	Y	y
	Ŝ	ŝ		
	Ŭ	ŭ		

Languages Overlapping with English

	Extra Letters		Omitted Letters
Spanish	Á	á	
	Ç	ç	
	É	é	
	Í	í	
	Ñ	ñ	
	Ó	ó	
	Ú	ú	
	Ü	ü	
Portuguese (Brazil)	Á	á	
	Â	â	
	Ã	ã	
	À	à	
	Ç	ç	
	É	é	
	Ê	ê	
	Í	í	
	Ó	ó	
	Ô	ô	
	Õ	õ	
	Ú	ú	

Languages Overlapping with English

	Extra Letters		Omitted Letters
French	À	à	
	Â	â	
	Æ	æ	
	Ç	ç	
	É	é	
	È	è	
	Ê	ê	
	Ë	ë	
	Î	î	
	Ï	ï	
	Ô	ô	
	Œ	œ	
	Ù	ù	
	Û	û	
	Ü	ü	
	Ÿ	ÿ	
German	Ä	ä	
	Ö	ö	
	Ü	ü	
	ß		
Dutch			

6

Languages Overlapping with English

	Extra Letters		Omitted Letters	
Swedish	Å	å		
	Ä	ä		
	Ö	ö		
Finnish	Å	å	W	w
	Ä	ä		
	Ö	ö		
Norwegian	Å	å		
	Æ	æ		
	Ø	ø		
Danish	Å	å		
	Æ	æ		
	Ø	ø		

Languages Overlapping with English

	Extra Letters		Omitted Letters	
Icelandic	Á	á	C	c
	Ð	ð	Q	q
	É	é	W	w
	Í	í	Z	z
	Ó	ó		
	Ú	ú		
	Ý	ý		
	Þ	þ		
	Æ	æ		
	Ö	ö		
Polish	Ą	ą	Q	q
	Ć	ć	V	v
	Ę	ę	X	x
	Ł	ł		
	Ń	ń		
	Ó	ó		
	Ś	ś		
	Ź	ź		
	Ż	ż		

Languages Overlapping with English

	Extra Letters		Omitted Letters	
Hungarian	Á	á	Q	q
	Cs	cs	W	w
	Dz	dz	X	x
	Dzs	Dzs	Y	y
	É	é		
	Gy	gy		
	Í	í		
	Ly	ly		
	Ó	ó		
	Ö	ö		
	Ő	ő		
	Ú	ú		
	Ü	ü		
	Ű	ű		

Languages Overlapping with English

	Extra Letters		Omitted Letters
Czech	Á	á	
	Č	č	
	Ď	ď	
	É	é	
	Ě	ě	
	Ch	ch	
	Í	í	
	Ň	ň	
	Ó	ó	
	Ř	ř	
	Š	š	
	Ú	ú	
	Ů	ů	
	Ý	ý	
	Ž	ž	

Languages Overlapping with English

	Extra Letters		Omitted Letters
Catalan	À	à	
	Ç	ç	
	É	é	
	È	è	
	Í	í	
	Ï	ï	
	Ó	ó	
	Ò	ò	
	Ú	ú	
	Ü	ü	
Galician	Á	á	
	Ç	ç	
	É	é	
	Í	í	
	Ñ	ñ	
	Ó	ó	
	Ú	ú	
Maltese	Ċ	ċ	
	Ġ	ġ	
	Ħ	ħ	
	Ż	ż	
Basque	Ñ	ñ	

Languages from Eastern Europe
& Middle Asia

Greek

A	α	Ξ	ξ
B	β	O	o
Γ	γ	Π	π
Δ	δ	P	ρ
E	ε	ς	ς
Z	ζ	Σ	σ
H	η	T	τ
Θ	θ	Y	υ
I	ι	Φ	φ
K	κ	X	χ
Λ	λ	Ψ	ψ
M	μ	Ω	ω
N	ν		

Russian

А	а		Р	р
Б	б		С	с
В	в		Т	т
Г	г		У	у
Д	д		Ф	ф
Е	е		Х	х
Ё	ё		Ц	ц
Ж	ж		Ч	ч
З	з		Ш	ш
И	и		Щ	щ
Й	й		Ъ	ъ
К	к		Ы	ы
Л	л		Ь	ь
М	м		Э	э
Н	н		Ю	ю
О	о		Я	я
П	п			

Ukrainian

А	а		Н	н
Б	б		О	о
В	в		П	п
Г	г		Р	р
Ґ	ґ		С	с
Д	д		Т	т
Е	е		У	у
Є	є		Ф	ф
Ж	ж		Х	х
З	з		Ц	ц
И	и		Ч	ч
Й	й		Ш	ш
І	і		Щ	щ
Ї	ї		Ь	ь
К	к		Ю	ю
Л	л		Я	я
М	м			

Bulgarian

А	а		Р	р
Б	б		С	с
В	в		Т	т
Г	г		У	у
Д	д		Ф	ф
Е	е		Х	х
Ж	ж		Ц	ц
З	з		Ч	ч
И	и		Ш	ш
Й	й		Щ	щ
К	к		Ъ	ъ
Л	л		Ь	ь
М	м		Э	э
Н	н		Ю	ю
О	о		Я	я
П	п			

Serbian

А	а		Н	н
Б	б		Њ	њ
В	в		О	о
Г	г		П	п
Д	д		Р	р
Ђ	ђ		С	с
Е	е		Т	т
Ж	ж		Ћ	ћ
З	з		У	у
Ѕ	ѕ		Ф	ф
И	и		Х	х
Ј	ј		Ц	ц
К	к		Ч	ч
Л	л		Џ	џ
Љ	љ		Ш	ш
М	м			

Macedonian

А	а		М	м
Б	б		Н	н
В	в		Њ	њ
Г	г		О	о
Ѓ	ѓ		П	п
Д	д		Р	р
Е	е		С	с
Ж	ж		Т	т
З	з		У	у
Ѕ	ѕ		Ф	ф
И	и		Х	х
Ј	ј		Ц	ц
К	к		Ч	ч
Ќ	ќ		Џ	џ
Л	л		Ш	ш
Љ	љ			

Belarusian

А	а		П	п
Б	б		Р	р
В	в		С	с
Г	г		Т	т
Д	д		У	у
Е	е		Ў	ў
Ё	ё		Ф	ф
Ж	ж		Х	х
З	з		Ц	ц
Й	й		Ч	ч
І	і		Ш	ш
К	к		Ы	ы
Л	л		Ь	ь
М	м		Э	э
Н	н		Ю	ю
О	о		Я	я

Georgian

ა	ლ	ფ
ბ	მ	ქ
გ	ნ	ყ
დ	ო	ც
ე	პ	წ
ვ	რ	ხ
ზ	ს	ჯ
თ	ტ	ჰ
კ	უ	

Armenian

Ա	ա	Կ	կ	Ս	ս
Բ	բ	Հ	հ	Վ	վ
Գ	գ	Ձ	ձ	Տ	տ
Դ	դ	Ղ	ղ	Ր	ր
Ե	ե	Ճ	ճ	Ց	g
Զ	զ	Մ	մ	Ի	ւ
Է	է	Յ	յ	Փ	փ
Ը	ը	Ն	ն	Ք	ք
Թ	թ	Շ	շ	Օ	o
Ժ	ժ	Ո	ո	Ֆ	ֆ
Ի	ի	Չ	չ		
Լ	լ	Պ	պ		
Խ	խ	Ջ	ջ		
Ծ	ծ	Ռ	ռ		

Languages Overlapping with English

	Extra Letters		Omitted Letters
Slovak	Á	á	
	Ä	ä	
	Č	č	
	Ď	ď	
	DŽ	dž	
	Ch	ch	
	É	é	
	Í	í	
	Ĺ	ĺ	
	Ľ	ľ	
	Ň	ň	
	Ó	ó	
	Ô	ô	
	Ŕ	ŕ	
	Š	š	
	Ť	ť	
	Ú	ú	
	Ý	ý	
	Ž	ž	

Languages Overlapping with English

	Extra Letters		Omitted Letters	
Slovenian	Č	č	Q	q
	Š	š	W	w
	Ž	ž	X	x
			Y	y
Bosnian	Ć	ć	Q	q
	Č	č	W	w
	Dž	dž	X	x
	Đ	đ	Y	y
	Lj	lj		
	Nj	nj		
	Š	š		
	Ž	ž		
Croatian	Ć	ć	Q	q
	Č	č	W	w
	Dž	dž	X	x
	Đ	đ	Y	y
	Lj	lj		
	Nj	nj		
	Š	š		
	Ž	ž		

Languages Overlapping with English

	Extra Letters		Omitted Letters	
Albanian (Originally Cyrillic)	Ç	ç	W	w
	Dh	dh		
	Ë	ë		
	Gj	gj		
	Ll	ll		
	Lj	lj		
	Nj	nj		
	Rr	rr		
	Sh	sh		
	Th	th		
	Xh	xh		
	Zh	zh		
Azerbaijani	Ç	ç	W	w
	Ə	ə		
	Ğ	ğ		
	İ	i		
	Ö	ö		
	Ş	ş		
	Ü	ü		

Languages Overlapping with English

	Extra Letters		Omitted Letters	
Latvian	Ā	ā	Q	q
	Č	č	W	w
	Ē	ē	X	x
	Ģ	ģ	Y	y
	Ī	ī		
	Ķ	ķ		
	Ļ	ļ		
	Ņ	ņ		
	Š	š		
	Ū	ū		
	Ž	ž		
Lithuanian	Ą	ą	Q	q
	Č	č	W	w
	Ę	ę	X	x
	Ė	ė		
	Į	į		
	Š	š		
	Ų	ų		
	Ū	ū		
	Ž	ž		

Languages Overlapping with English

	Extra Letters		Omitted Letters	
Estonian	Š	š	C	c
	Ž	ž	Q	q
	Õ	õ	W	w
	Ä	ä	X	x
	Ö	ö	Y	y
	Ü	ü		
Romanian	Ă	ă		
	Â	â		
	Î	î		
	Ș	ș		
	Ț	ț		

Languages from the Middle East
& Pakistan

Hebrew

א מ

ב ן

ג ס

ד ע

ה פ

ו ף

ז ץ

ח צ

ט ק

י ר

ך ש

כ ת

ל

ם

Yiddish

מ   א

ן   ב

ס   ג

ע   ד

פ   ה

פ   ו

צ   ז

ץ   ח

ק   ט

ר   י

ש   כ

ת   ל

       ם

Arabic

غ	ت	ذ
ف	ث	٠
ق	ج	١
ك	ح	٢
ل	خ	٣
لا	د	٤
م	ر	٥
ن	ز	٦
ه	س	٧
و	ش	٨
ؤ	ص	٩
ى	ض	ء
ي	ط	ا
ئ	ظ	ب
	ع	ة

Persian

غ ف
ق ک
گ ل
م ن
ه و
ی

ج چ
ح خ
د ذ
ر ز
س ش
ص ض
ط ظ
ع

۰ ۱
۲ ۳
۴ ۵
۶ ۷
۸ ۹
۱
ب پ
ت ث

Urdu

Languages Overlapping with English

	Extra Letters		Omitted Letters	
Turkish	Ç	ç	Q	q
	Ğ	ğ	W	w
	İ	i	X	x
	Ö	ö		
	Ş	ş		
	Ü	ü		

Languages from Eastern Asia

Japanese

るれろワわヰゐヱゑヲをんミニオ

マまみムむめモもヤやユゆョよラらリりルル

とナなにヌぬネねノのハはヒひフふヘホほ

こサさしスすセせソそタたチちっツてテ

。＾テアあイいウエえおカかキきクくケけコ

35

Japanese

キヤ	ちょ	みや
きや	ツヤ	みゆ
きゅ	ツユ	みよ
キユ	ツヨ	リヤ
キヨ	ニヤ	りや
さよ	にや	りゅ
しや	にゆ	リユ
しゅ	によ	りょ
しょ	ヒヤ	リヨ
チヤ	ひや	ミヤ
ちや	ヒュ	ミュ
チュ	ひゅ	ミヨ
ちゅ	ヒヨ	ニュ
チョ	ひよ	ニヨ

Korean

ㄱ ㄴ ㄷ ㄹ ㅁ ㅂ ㅅ ㅇ ㅈ ㅊ ㅋ ㅌ ㅍ

ㅎ ㅏ ㅐ ㅑ ㅓ ㅔ ㅕ ㅗ ㅛ ㅜ ㅠ ㅡ ㅣ

Mandarin Chinese
(Word Selection)

日	去	喝
月	真	付
字	吸	吃
人	嘆	喝
屋	睡	付
市	晨	雞
車	學	腿
街	讀	茶
場	愛	水

Cantonese
(Word Selection)

行	好	雞
食	請	牛
飲	遲	魚
睇	早	蛋
點	左	麵
似	右	飯
仲	去	豆
講	晏	茶
話	鹽	水

Languages from Southeast Asia

Thai

๐	◌ํ	ค	ณ	ย	◌ั
๑	◌ั	ฅ	ด	ร	า
๒	◌ํ	ฆ	ต	ฤ	◌ำ
๓	"	ง	ถ	ล	โิ
๔	,	จ	ท	ฦ	◌ี
๕	/	ฉ	ธ	ว	◌ึ
๖	฿	ช	น	ศ	◌ื
๗	เ	ซ	บ	ษ	◌ุ
๘	แ	ฌ	ป	ส	◌ู
๙	โ	ญ	ผ	ห	◌ฺ
-	ใ	ฎ	ฝ	พ	ๅ
◌่	ไ	ฏ	พ	อ	ๆ
◌้	ก	ฐ	ฟ	ฮ	
◌๊	ข	ฑ	ภ	ฯ	
◌๋	ฃ	ฒ	ม	ะ	

41

Lao

ໍ   ໆ   ວ   ເ

ົ   ຫ   ຫ   ແ

ກ   ນ   ອ   ໂ

ຂ   ບ   ຮ   ໍ

ຄ   ປ   ະ   ໄ

ງ   ຜ   າ   ໃ

ຈ   ຝ   ເ   ໍາ

ຊ   ພ   ແ   ໍ

ຍ   ຟ   ໂ   ໍ

ດ   ມ   ໃ

ຕ   ຢ   ໄ

ຖ   ຣ   ໍ

Khmer

ឳ ក ឈ ឱ ៅ

ក ខ ញ ឹ ំ

ខ ទ ស ុំ ៈ

គ ឃ ឡ ុះ ៍

ឃ ប ឣ ើ ៌

ង ផ ឞ ៀ ៎

ច ឰ ទ ៀ ៕

ឆ ម ៉ ែ ៚

ឈ ៊ ៊ េះ ៗ

ញ ្ ៗ ោ

ឌ ្ឫ ាំ ោ

ណ ្ឭ ិ ៅ

ឝ ី ៅះ

Languages Overlapping with English

	Extra Letters		Omitted Letters	
Vietnamese	Ă	ă	F	f
	Â	â	J	j
	Đ	đ	W	w
	Ê	ê	Z	z
	Ô	ô		
	Ơ	ơ		
	Ư	ư		

Languages from South Asia

Bengali

ঃ	ন	ি
ঁং	প	ী
ক	ব	ু
গ	ম	ূ
চ	য	ৃ
জ	র	ে
ট	ল	ৈ
ড	স	ো
ত	হ	ৌ
দ	া	্

Hindi

◌ः	ब	◌ॢ
◌ं	म	◌ृ
क	य	◌े
ग	र	◌ै
च	ल	◌ॉ
ज	व	◌ो
ट	स	◌ौ
ड	ह	◌ॆ
त	ण	
द	ि	
न	ी	
प	ु	

Marathi

न	ऋ	ज्ञ	न	पो	ळ
अ	ए	ट	प	पौ	व
अँ	ऐ	ठ	पं	फ	श्र
अं	ओ	ड	पः	ब	ष
अः	औ	ड.	पा	भ	ह
आ	क	ढ	पि	म	◌ं
आँ	क्ष	ण	पी	य	
इ	ग	त	पु	र	
इ	घ	त्त	पू	र्	
ई	छ	थ	पृ	रन	
उ	ज	द	पे	रा	
ऊ	झ	ध	पै	ल	

Punjabi

ਉ	ਤ	ਓ
ਅ	ਦ	ਇ
ਸ	ਨ	ਈ
ਹ	ਪ	ਉ
ਕ	ਬ	ਊ
ਗ	ਮ	ਏ
ਚ	ਯ	ਐ
ਜ	ਰ	ਓ
ਟ	ਲ	ਔ
ਡ	ਵ	ਅ

Nepali

ज्ञ	औ	य
०	क	र
१	ख	र्
२	ग	ल
३	च	व
४	ज	श
५	त	ष
६	त्र	स
७	थ	ह
८	द	ण ि␣
९	ध	ृ ु ो
ा	न	ॆ
ः	प	
S	ब	
अ	भ	
उ	म	

50

Gujarati

૦ઃ	પ	◌ી
◌ં◌ઁ	બ	◌ુ
ક	મ	◌ૂ
ગ	ય	◌ૃ
ચ	ર	◌ે
જ	લ	◌ૈ
ટ	વ	◌ો
ડ	સ	◌ૌ
ત	હ	◌ૅ
દ	◌ળ	
ન	િ◌	

Tamil

◌ஂ	ர	◌ு
க	ல	◌ூ
ச	வ	◌ெ
ட	ஜ	◌ே
த	ஸ	◌ை
ந	ஹ	◌ொ
ப	◌ா	◌ோ
ம	◌ி	◌ௌ
ய	◌ீ	◌்

Telugu

ం	బ	ఒ
క	మ	ఓ
గ	య	ఋ
చ	ర	ఐ
జ	ల	ఏ
ట	వ	ఔ
డ	స	ఓ
త	హ	ఔ
ద	ఔ	ఔ
న	ఇ	
ప	ఈ	

53

Kannada

ಂ	ಬ	ಲಿ
ಕ	ಮ	ೂ
ಗ	ಯ	ೃ
ಚ	ರ	ೆ
ಜ	ಲ	ೇ
ಟ	ವ	ೈ
ಡ	ಸ	ೊ
ತ	ಹ	ೋ
ದ	ೌ	ೌ
ನ	ೊ	ೕ
ಪ	ೋ	

Languages from the Oceans

Languages Overlapping with English

	Extra Letters		Omitted Letters	
Indonesian				
Javanese				
Malay				
Filipino	Ñ NG	ñ ng		
Cebuano	NG	ng	C F J Q V X Z	c f j q v x z
Haitian	À Ch Ç É È Ng Ù	à ch ç é è ng ù	C Q X	c q x

Languages from Africa

Languages Overlapping with English

	Extra Letters		Omitted Letters	
Afrikaans				
Swahili				
Hausa				
Igbo				
Yoruba				
Zulu				
Somali	DH KH SH		P V Z	p v z

Neo-Tifinagh Berber Glyphs
(Selection)

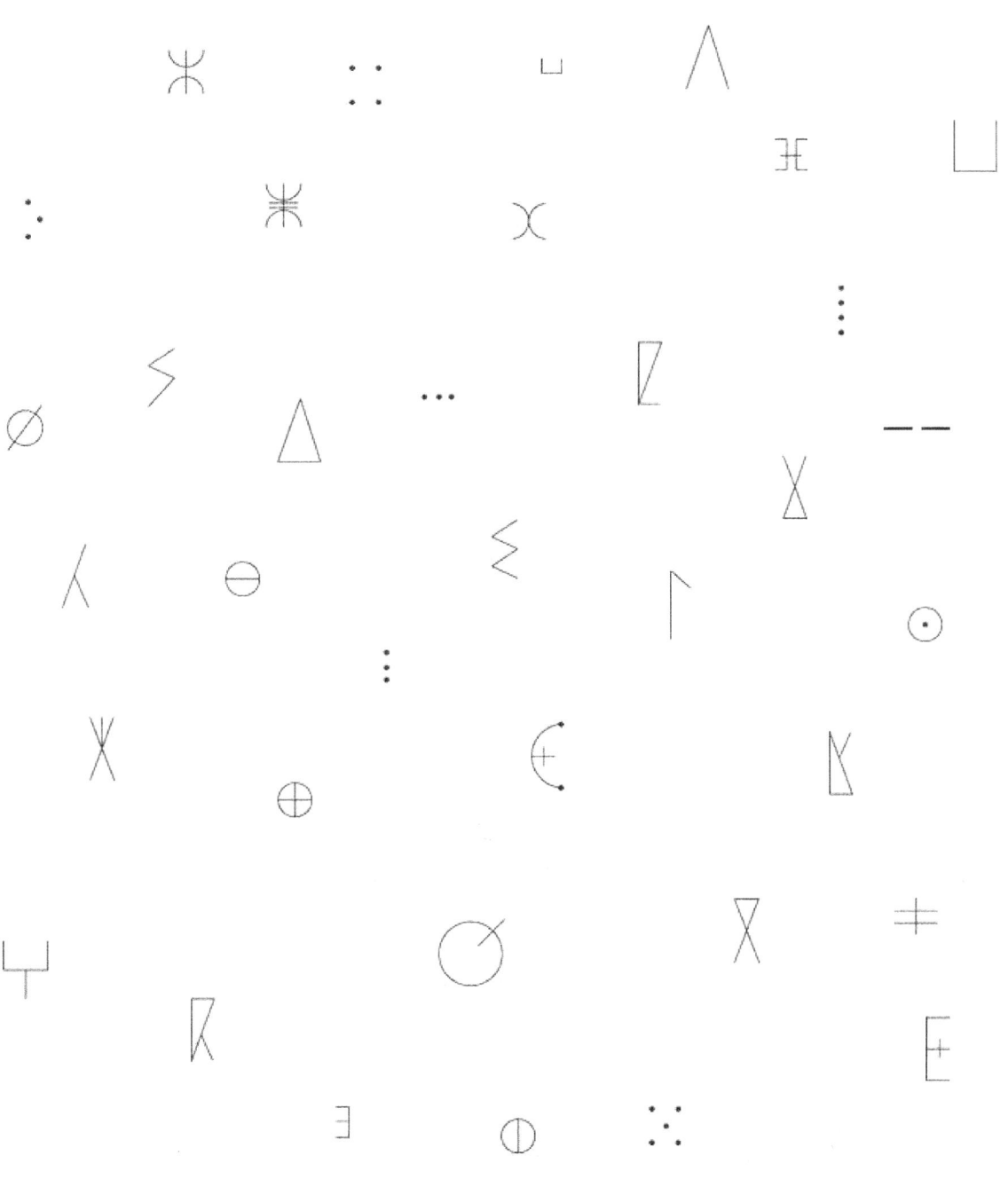

Ancient Egyptian Hieroglypics
(Selection)

References

Translate.Google.com

Wikipedia.org

.

About the Author

An award-winning musician and science student as a youth and young adult, M. Schottenbauer, Ph.D., studied music, physics, mathematics, and liberal arts at the university before going on to earn a doctorate in psychology. Dr. Schottenbauer held a position as a Research Assistant Professor, and currently works as an independent educational consultant.

Printed in Great Britain
by Amazon

23097877R00040